Native American Tribes: The History and Culture of the Cherokee

By Charles River Editors

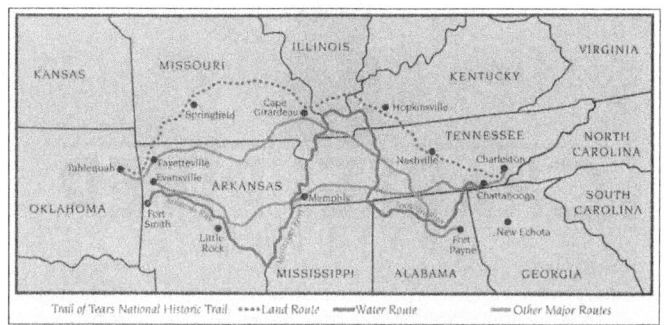

The Trail of Tears route

About Charles River Editors

Charles River Editors was founded by Harvard and MIT alumni to provide superior editing and original writing services, with the expertise to create digital content for publishers across a vast range of subject matter. In addition to providing original digital content for third party publishers, Charles River Editors republishes civilization's greatest literary works, bringing them to a new generation via ebooks.

Sign up here to receive updates about free books as we publish them, and visit Our Kindle Author Page to browse today's free promotions and our most recently published Kindle titles.

Introduction

Cherokee beadwork

The Cherokee

"We are overwhelmed! Our hearts are sickened, our utterance is paralyzed, when we reflect on the condition in which we are placed, by the audacious practices of unprincipled men, who have managed their stratagems with so much dexterity as to impose on the Government of the United States, in the face of our earnest, solemn, and reiterated protestations." – Principal Chief John Ross

From the "Trail of Tears" to Wounded Knee and Little Bighorn, the narrative of American history is incomplete without the inclusion of the Native Americans that lived on the continent before European settlers arrived in the 16th and 17th centuries. Since the first contact between natives and settlers, tribes like the Sioux, Cherokee, and Navajo have both fascinated and perplexed outsiders with their history, language, and culture. In Charles River Editors' Native American Tribes series, readers can get caught up to speed on the history and culture of North America's most famous native tribes in the time it takes to finish a commute, while learning interesting facts long forgotten or never known.

Tragically, the Cherokee is one of America's best known tribes due to the trials and tribulations they suffered by being forcibly moved west along the "Trail of Tears", but that overlooks the contributions they made to American society well before the 19th century. The Cherokee began the process of assimilation into European America very early, even before the establishment of the Unites States, and by the early 19th century they were one of the "Five

Civilized Tribes."

Ultimately, however, it is unclear what benefits "civilization" brought the tribe. Throughout the colonial period and after the American Revolution, the Cherokee struggled to satisfy the whims and desires of American government officials and settlers, often suffering injustices after complying with their desires. Nevertheless, the Cherokee continued to endure, and after being pushed west, they rose from humble origins as refugees new to the southeastern United States to build themselves back up into a powerhouse both economically and militarily. Even after being forced to leave their traditional homeland again, they once more rose to become a powerful tribe and nation, ruling themselves and building their economic power through wise and skillful leadership.

Despite all of the hostilities, the Cherokee ultimately became the first people of non-European descent to become U.S. citizens en masse, and today the Cherokee Nation is the largest federally recognized tribe in the United States, boasting over 300,000 members. Given what they overcame in the last 200 years, the story of the Cherokee Nation is a testament to the resiliency, cohesiveness, and power of the Cherokee people. *Native American Tribes: The History and Culture of the Cherokee* comprehensively covers the culture and history of the famous tribe, profiling their origins, their famous leaders, and their lasting legacy. Along with pictures of important people, places, and events, you will learn about the Cherokee like you never have before, in no time at all.

Native American Tribes: The History and Culture of the Cherokee
About Charles River Editors
Introduction
   Chapter 1: The Cherokee Creation Story
   Chapter 2: Historical Origins of the Cherokee
   Chapter 3: Fighting the Europeans and Other Tribes
   Chapter 4: Cherokee Society
   Chapter 5: The Cherokee Religion
   Chapter 6: Cherokee Nation v. Georgia
   Chapter 7: The Trail of Tears
   Chapter 8: The Aftermath
   Eyewitness John Burnett's Account of the Trail of Tears
   The Cherokee Constitution of 1839
   Bibliography

Chapter 1: The Cherokee Creation Story

"These formulas furnish a complete refutation of the assertion so frequently made by ignorant and prejudiced writers that the Indian had no religion excepting what they are pleased to call the meaning less mummeries of the medicine man. This is the very reverse of the truth. The Indian is essentially religious and contemplative and it might almost be said that every act of his life is regulated and determined by his religious belief. It matters not that some may call this superstition. The difference is only relative. The religion of to-day has developed from the cruder superstitions of yesterday, and Christianity itself is but an outgrowth and enlargement of the beliefs and ceremonies which have been preserved by the Indian in their more ancient form. When we are willing to admit that the Indian has a religion which he holds sacred, even though it be different from our own, we can then admire the consistency of the theory, the particularity of the ceremonial and the beauty of the expression." – James Mooney

In his book *Black Elk Speaks* (John G. Neihardt's transcription of Black Elk's description of Lakota spiritual beliefs), the author quotes Black Elk, who asserted that all Native American peoples believed in a single god. For the Sioux, this concept was referred to as Wakan Tanka (Great Mystery), and near the end of his life, Black Elk – a convert to Christianity – voiced a belief that the idea of the "Great Spirit" present in many Native American belief systems referred to the same deity referred to in the Judeo-Christian tradition. For the Cherokee, the term "Great One" refers to the principle guiding spirit of the tribe.

According to the Cherokee's foundational narrative, in the distant past the tribe's spirit people were originally in the "sky vault." This vault began to get crowded with the spirit versions of the Cherokee, and "The Great One" decided that the time had come for the sky vault to be extended to the earth and for the Cherokee to be given physical bodies. The Great One conducted a council of all the spirit Cherokee people so they could discuss the transition and decide on a plan. During the course of the council, the Great One charged those spirit beings who chose to settle on Mother Earth in physical bodies with protecting and acting as stewards over her. The guiding spirit also gave the Cherokee people authority over the secrets of Mother Earth and the responsibility of protecting all the living things that chose to live on Earth. Also, the Cherokee were given the "power medicine" of free will to perform these protective and stewardship duties. Finally, the Great One told the Cherokee that other tribes would follow them to live upon the Earth, and that they would also receive the gift of free will to be keepers of the Earth and its inhabitants as well.

According to the Cherokee, in the distant past the Earth was like an island in a great expanse of water, suspended by four sacred "Cords of Life." According to the Great One, the Earth-island existed in perfect balance hanging on the sacred cords, and it would be dependent upon the various tribes of beings living on it. In this case, "tribes" refers not only to human tribes but was outlined by the Great One to include the various tribes of animals in addition to humans. The tribes were distinguished by their respective number of legs: no-legged, two-legged, four-legged, and many-legged tribes. In the creation account, members of the animal tribes were the first to take physical form and begin exploring and colonizing the Earth.

The first to venture forth was the Water Beetle, grandchild of the beaver, who flew about seeking a place to land. Water Beetle found no dry land and continually foundered in the water, drawing up his muddy feet. The droplets of mud that fell from his feet became islands in the sea. Members of the bird clan volunteered to venture forth next, citing their ability to fly about over great distances. Great Buzzard flew down to the Earth, but because of his great size, his wings frequently struck the surface of the water, stirring up mud and creating valleys and mountains. Finally, Great Buzzard returned to his home in the sky vault.

After the efforts of the Water Beetle and Great Buzzard the Earth had dried, and the Fish Clan offered to go down to the Earth to stay. Some of the Fish Clan wanted to stay on land though, and they became known as the Crawfish. After crawling up onto the red clay of the Earth, the Crawfish was baked in the sun and was thereafter known as the Red Crawfish. According to the legend, the seventh day saw some members of the Animal Clan who had hidden under the surface of the Earth come up to have a look around. They were the worms, and after coming up to the surface they were badly burned and were afterwards known as the Red Worms. The great heat caused the members of the Animal Clan to call on the Great One for help.

Hearing the calls of the Animal Clan, the Great One came down to Earth on the seventh day, bringing lovely plants and trees to provide air for the Cherokee people. Being unused to their physical bodies and breathing, the Cherokee people rested on the first day. After that day, they worked for the next six days, resting during the nights, just as the Sun did. Being proud of the Cherokee, the Great One asked the Thunder Beings to ignite a tree with their lightening and thus provide the people with the warmth of the Sacred Fire. This series of events established the way that all the clans, animals, insects, birds, trees, plants, and humans would conduct ceremonies around the Sacred Fire to demonstrate their respect and love for the living Mother Earth.

19th century ethnographer James Mooney collected Cherokee manuscripts and later published *History, Myths, and Sacred Formulas of the Cherokees*, and his work included an official account of the Cherokee creation story:

"When all was water, the animals lived above in Galunlati but it was very crowded and they wanted more room. Dayunisi, the little Water-beetle, offered to go see what was below the water. It repeatedly dived to the bottom and came up with soft mud eventually forming the island we call earth. The island was suspended by cords at each of the cardinal points to the sky vault, which is solid rock.

Birds were sent down to find a dry place to live but none could be found. The Great Buzzard, the father of all buzzards we see now, flew down close to the earth while it was still soft. He became tired and his wings began to strike the ground. Where they struck the earth became a valley and where they rose up again became a mountain and thus the Cherokee country was created.

The animals came down after the earth dried but all was dark so they set the sun in a track to go every day across the island from east to west. At first the sun was too close to the island and too hot. They raised the sun again and again, seven times, until it was the right height just under the sky arch. The highest place, Gulkwagine Digalunlatiyun, is 'the seventh height'.

The animals and plants were told to keep watch for seven nights but as the days passed many begin to fall asleep until on the seventh night only the owl, panther, and a couple of others were still awake. These were given the power to see in the dark and prey on the birds and animals that sleep at night. Of the plants, only the cedar, the pine, the spruce, the holly, and the laurel were awake to the end and were therefore given the power to be always green and to be the greatest medicine, but to the others it was said: 'Because you have not endured to the end you shall lose your hair every winter.'

Men came after animals and plants. At first there were only a brother and sister until he struck her with a fish and told her to multiply, and so it was. In seven days a child was born to her and thereafter every seven days another until there was danger that the world could not keep up with them. Then it was made that a woman should have only one child in a year, and it has been so ever since."

This creation story helped explain to the Cherokee why their settlements were located near the Great Smoky Mountains along the Tennessee-North Carolina border.

The first man and woman to occupy the Earth were named Kanati and Selu respectively. The first woman, Selu, is also sometimes called the Corn Mother because she gave birth to the corn plants that would sustain the Cherokee people. The first couple had one son, and later they had a second son who was born from the blood of the animals Kanati had hunted for their sustenance. At that time, all the game animals were trapped in a great cave, and Kanati rolled away the great stone blocking the entrance everyday to release a few animals he could then hunt and kill to feed his family. After the hunt, he dutifully rolled the stone back into place.

Selu, the Corn Mother, produced corn for the family by growing it out of her body. One day, her two sons killed their mother and dragged her body across the country, causing corn to sprout from the furrow formed by her body. The two boys then rolled the stone away from the mouth of the cave holding all the animals, releasing them all at once. The first couple moved to the west after this. Their sons moved even further to the west, and their voices can be heard as the thunder roaring from storms that come from the western skies.

Chapter 2: Historical Origins of the Cherokee

Like many Native American tribes, the Cherokee experienced "forced migrations," both at the hands of their fellow indigenous people and most infamously, during the Trail of Tears episode when they were forced from their homeland by the U.S. military. As a result, the Cherokee are often associated with the Deep South, but originally, the Cherokee lived in the northeastern part of the present-day United States, around the Great Lakes. At some time in the distant past, the tribe was forced out of the region, probably at the hands of a militarily stronger tribe. While it has long been believed that it was the Iroquois who forced the Cherokee to migrate south and settle in the present-day southeastern United States. Delaware tribal legends support the defeat of the Cherokee but Iroquois legends make no mention of such a story.

Today it is believed that the Cherokee migrated south thousands of years ago. The Cherokee language is part of the Iroquoian language family but has changed significantly, indicating that the tribe left its ancestral homeland at least several millennia ago. Glottochronology is an anthropological technique of tracking linguistic changes in related languages to determine how long people groups sharing the root language have been separated. The technique studies core words and attempts to decipher the length of time needed to achieve perceived changes. Using this technique, researchers have estimated that the Cherokee departed from the Iroquois ancestors about 6,000 years ago. However, because language does not leave archaeological evidence, this estimate is far from certain.

The name Cherokee is likely derived from the Creek word chelokee, which means "people of a different speech." Also, though many Cherokee people accept the term "Cherokee," some prefer and use the word "Tsalagi" to refer to themselves and their tribe. Originally, the Cherokee referred to themselves as the Aniyunwiya or Anniyaya which can be translated as "the principal people. This moniker understandably fits with the Cherokee creation narrative, in which the Cherokee are the first (among many) Native American tribes to occupy the Earth. They also called themselves the Keetoowah, meaning the "people of Kituhwa." Other indigenous tribes had names for the Cherokee, many of which resemble Cherokee, Tsalagi, and Keetoohwa. A few examples are: Chilukki (used by the Choctaw and Chickasaw and meaning "dog people"), Talligewi (used by the Delaware people), and Kittuwa (used by the Algonquin people).

From their northeastern origins, the Cherokee migrated to the present-day southeastern United States to settle in a region currently composed of parts of western North and South Carolina, Northern Georgia, southwestern Virginia, and the Cumberland Basin of Tennessee, Kentucky, and northern Alabama. While the tribe's population prior to European contact remains unknown, it is estimated that epidemics beginning in 1540 (the date of first contact with the DeSoto Expedition) likely killed at least 75% of the tribe's population. By 1674, the Cherokee had rebounded to about 50,000 members, but a series of epidemics in 1729, 1738, and 1753 further reduced this number by half. Just prior to their removal in the late 1830s, the population was around 25,000 and relatively stable.

The Cherokee tribe has traditionally been divided into three sub-groups based upon location and the distinct dialect of the Cherokee language. The Lower Cherokee lived in the eastern-most villages, and the Over-the-Hill Cherokee were those who occupied the western-most towns. As their designation implies, the Middle Cherokee occupied the territory between the two aforementioned groups. In addition to these three groups, several other distinctive bands of Cherokee people are identified as the Chickamauga, Onnontiogg, and Qualia. Also identified are two bands – the Atali and the Etali – whose names suggest that they may be one band that was given two different names by those who recorded them.

Chapter 3: Fighting the Europeans and Other Tribes

Hernando de Soto

The first contact with Cherokee people made by Europeans occurred in 1540, when members of the de Soto Expedition recorded that they had found "Chalaque" settlements along the Tennessee River. The Spanish established and maintained a small mining and smelting operation that remained in the region until around 1690, but because the Cherokee generally lived in remote mountainous regions, they were able to avoid frequent contact with European settlers until about 1609, when the colony of Virginia was established.

By 1629, English settlers had entered the Appalachian Mountains and came into contact with Cherokee villages, and after the founding of the Carolina colonies, European contact with the Cherokee became almost constant. An expedition sent by Virginia-based trader Abraham Wood established a trading network with Cherokee living in their capital at Echota in present-day northern Alabama in 1673. Though Virginia traders attempted to maintain a monopoly on the lucrative trade in animal skins and Native American slaves with the Cherokee, the enterprising indigenous group approached newcomers from the Carolinas and established trade connections with them the following year as well. Traders from South Carolina established a treaty with Cherokee living in their area by 1684, and a steady flow of deerskins and slaves began to flow out of the Cherokee villages.

During this time, life among the Cherokee inevitably began to change as well. As contact with colonial traders increased, the level of dependence on European goods increased among the Cherokee. Moreover, the political power base within the Cherokee settlements shifted from the priest/shaman class to that of the hunter/warrior as the latter became "hunters for profit." The increasing reliance on European goods from the English colonies also caused the Cherokee to ally themselves with the English against the Spanish and French during conflicts between 1689 and 1763. This was a natural byproduct of the fact that Cherokee warriors raided Spanish settlements in present-day northern Florida in the 1670s, and they were also fighting with the coastal tribes in the Carolinas.

The frequent warring between the Native American tribes was exacerbated by the fact that the Europeans introduced superior military technology to them upon their arrival. By 1680, most tribes in the region had acquired firearms, forcing the larger Cherokee settlements throughout the region to become more militarized and fortified against attack. Also during this period, conflicts with the Catawba to the east and the Choctaw and Creek to the south escalated until the tribes were engaged in almost constant fighting. Traditional enmity with the Chickasaw, another Native American tribe allied with the British, also kept the Cherokee busy with fighting to the west. On top of all that, there were territory conflicts along the northern frontiers of Cherokee territory between English, French, and Dutch traders.

While the Cherokee fought their traditional enemies and the European conflict evolved into the Beaver Wars, the expanding and powerful Iroquois League pushed Native Americans out of the

Great Lakes, creating a stream of refugees that headed south and also came into contact with the Cherokee. As a result, during the mid-17th century, large numbers of Shawnee people were forced out of their traditional homelands by powerful Iroquois bands, and these refugees entered traditionally Cherokee territory. Taking advantage of the situation and essentially using the Shawnee as a buffer, the Cherokee allowed the refugees to settle between themselves and their regional enemies. One Shawnee group was allowed to settle in South Carolina between Cherokee towns and the Catawba tribe, and a second group was allowed to settle in the Cumberland Basin of Tennessee as a buffer between the Cherokee and the Chickasaw.

This decision eventually proved problematic for the Cherokee when the Iroquois, remembering their enemies, ventured south and raided Shawnee and Cherokee settlements. Eventually, the Shawnee grew into a threat to the Cherokee as well, and in the late 17th century, Shawnee raiders destroyed a major Cherokee town while raiding it for slaves because the village's warriors were away on a hunt. The raid destroyed the fragile trust that had existed between the Cherokee and Shawnee, and the following year a group of Cherokee leaders traveled to Charlestown and asked for additional firearms to defend their villages against raiders bent on capturing slaves for the lucrative South Carolina trade.

Attitudes among the Cherokee in the Carolinas were so dangerously inflammatory that during the first decade of the 18th century, North Carolina officials demanded that South Carolina traders curtail the Native American slave trade for fear of a general rebellion. British government officials eventually stepped in and brokered a peace treaty between the Iroquois and the Cherokee, and over the course of the next 10 years, Cherokee warriors allied with different partners – both colonials and fellow Native American tribes – to secure their region and rid themselves of common enemies. Still, the Shawnee problem remained, and in 1715 Cherokee warriors entered into an alliance with their old adversaries, the Chickasaw. Together, the two tribes dealt a crippling blow to the Shawnee in the Cumberland Basin, but their alliance attracted the attention of both the French traders and their Algonquin allies, who began a series of raids against Cherokee villages from strongholds north of the Ohio River.

This period of conflict would last until the middle of the 18th century, during which time the Cherokee found themselves fighting Native American allies of both the British (the Iroquois) and the French (the Algonquins). Finally, in 1745, the Cherokee again allied with the Chickasaw and drove the remaining Shawnee over the Ohio River and out of Cherokee territory for good. The alliance then turned on another common enemy and French ally, the Choctaw, and defeated them in 1750.

The first half of the 18th century also saw the first land ceded to white settlers by the Cherokee. In a treaty between British colonists and Cherokee tribal members in 1721, a boundary between Cherokee and British settlements was established, but North Carolina and South Carolina settlers were soon making incursions into Lower Cherokee territory east of the Appalachians anyway.

Additionally, French traders had established a trading post near Montgomery, Alabama in 1717 and made contact with the Over-the-Hill Cherokee by navigating along the Cumberland River. Many Cherokee were tempted to switch their allegiance from the British to the French, but practical realities dissuaded them. French goods were of lower quality than those provided by the British, and the British had the naval power to effectively cut off French colonies in Canada by blockading the northeast points of entry. Also, the Chickasaw made navigation on the Tennessee River, a major trading route, virtually impossible for the French.

The British, sensing that the Cherokee might be tempted by French offers of allegiance, sent representatives to regulate trade and streamline trade relations by urging the Cherokee to appoint a single chief for each town, and British influence also led to peace treaties between the Cherokee and their former enemies the Catawba and the Wyandot tribes. During these peace negotiations, the Cherokee learned that the Wyandot and other Native American tribes were secretly planning to abandon their trade alliances with the French, information that ended any further consideration of the French as a trade alternative to the British. In the end, the French were simply unable to compete with the British in terms of quality of goods and access to Native American trading partners.

At the same time, the British remained concerned that the Cherokee would switch alliances, and they weren't entirely concerned about maintaining their end of the land bargains they struck with the Cherokee. Throughout the remainder of the 18th century, the Cherokee lost land to British colonists invading and settling on their land, and the tribe alternated between fighting against them and for them.

During the American Revolution, the Cherokee sided with the British, and the decision cost them heavily. Cherokee war parties engaged in several unsuccessful raids against American settlements, and the colonists responded with several victories, forcing the Cherokee to sue for peace. In the ensuing peace negotiations, the Cherokee gave up their ancestral and historical claims to territory in North Carolina and South Carolina, codified in the Treaty of DeWitts Corner (1777) and the Treaties of Long Island of Holston drafted in 1777 and 1781. The defeats and the territorial concessions would induce the Cherokee to strive for assimilation into American society in the early 19th century.

Chapter 4: Cherokee Society

While the Cherokee's alliances and political situation remained constantly fluid, the structure of their society was relatively stable. Cherokee settlements were comprised of 30-60 houses and a large, central council house. Their primary structures were built by waddle and daub construction, a woven, dome-shaped framework of wood plastered over with mud. Council houses were often located on mounds remaining from the earlier Mississippian culture and used for councils, meetings, and religious rituals. The council houses were also home to the "sacred fire," a flame the Cherokee had kept burning since the beginning of time.

The Cherokee National Council Building in New Echota (Georgia), their capital

By the time the Europeans made contact with the tribe, the Cherokee were living in a settled agricultural society, cultivating the "holy trinity" of ancient American agriculture: corn, beans, and squash. Eaten together, these three vegetables form complex proteins and were the primary sources of food for several major civilizations in the Americas. The tribe augmented this diet with wild animals hunted in the wilderness surrounding their settlements and by gathering wild foodstuffs.

Like other tribes, the Cherokee also used their sources of food for other purposes, especially medical purposes. James Mooney documented how Cherokee shamans gathered plants and herbs and performed rituals that would give them special medicinal values:

"There are a number of ceremonies and regulations observed in connection with the gathering of the herbs, roots, and barks, which can not be given in detail within the limits of this paper. In searching for his medicinal plants the shaman goes provided with a number of white and red beads, and approaches the plant from a certain direction, going round it from right to left one or four times, reciting certain prayers the while. He then pulls up the plant by the roots and drops one of the beads into the hole and covers it up with the loose earth. In one of the formulas for hunting ginseng the hunter addresses the mountain as the "Great Man" and assures it that he comes only to take a small piece of flesh (the ginseng) from its side, so that it seems probable that the bead is intended as a compensation to the earth for the plant thus torn from her bosom. In some cases the doctor must pass by the first three plants met until he comes to the fourth, which he takes and may then return for the others. The bark is always taken from the east side of the tree, and when the root or branch is used it must also be one which runs out toward the east, the reason given being that these have imbibed more medical potency from the rays of the sun.

When the roots, herbs, and barks which enter into the prescription have been thus gathered the doctor ties them up into a convenient package, which he takes to a running stream and casts into the water with appropriate prayers. Should the package float, as it generally does, he accepts the fact as an omen that his treatment will be successful. On the other band, should it sink, he concludes that some part of the preceding ceremony has been improperly carried out and at once sets about procuring a new package, going over the whole performance from the beginning. Herb-gathering by moonlight, so important a feature in European folk medicine, seems to be no part of Cherokee ceremonial. There are fixed regulations in regard to the preparing of the decoction, the care of the medicine during the continuance of the treatment, and the disposal of what remains after the treatment is at an end. In the arrangement of details the shaman frequently employs the services of a lay assistant."

Cherokee society was constructed of kinship ties traced through seven seminal matrilineal clans. Membership in a specific clan was determined by the individual's mother, which closely resembles the tradition societal structure of other Iroquoian peoples. However, women in Cherokee society never reached the levels of influence enjoyed by Iroquoian women, and in most other ways, Cherokee society resembled that of other southeastern Native American tribes. Local chiefs or head-men led individual Cherokee towns, and the villages' inhabitants only gathered together with the entire tribe during religious ceremonies, celebrations, or war. Much like Native Americans elsewhere, the situation dictated which particular chief led the tribe. During times of war, "red" chiefs assumed leadership roles, while during peaceful times, "white" chiefs assumed leadership roles.

By the early 19th century, the Cherokee had actively begun trying to assimilate into U.S. society, the most notable byproduct of which was their written constitution (which can be found in the appendix). In their constitution, the tribe codified its governmental system and established both court and school systems. Many members of the tribe also converted to Christianity, and white missionaries lived among them unhindered. In fact, the tribe's rapid advancement and relative affluence made their white neighbors envious of the Cherokee's standard of living.

In 1821, Sequoyah (also known as George Gist) developed a writing system for the Cherokee language. Using a system of 86 symbols, each with a phonetic value, Sequoyah assigned syllabic values to each symbol that represented all the sounds used while speaking the Cherokee language. Because the system was relatively simple and easy to learn, the vast majority of Cherokee people became literate in their native tongue within a few years. Furthermore, *The*

Phoenix, a Cherokee language newspaper, began publication in February 1828. Due to these early efforts to assimilate into U.S. society and adopt practices, the Cherokee remain one of the most highly educated Native American tribes and maintain one of the highest standards of living among indigenous peoples.

A lithograph based off a portrait of Sequoya

Chapter 5: The Cherokee Religion

Like other Native American tribes, the Cherokee had a very complex religion. James Mooney wrote about their belief system, and how the Cherokee invoked their gods and practiced their religion:

> "The religion of the Cherokees, like that of most of our North American tribes, is zootheism or animal worship, with the survival of that earlier stage designated by Powell as hecastotheism, or the worship of all things tangible, and the beginnings of a higher system in which the elements and the great powers of nature are deified. Their pantheon includes gods in the heaven above, on the earth beneath, and in the waters under the earth, but of these the animal gods constitute by far the most numerous class, although the elemental gods are more important. Among the animal gods insects and

fishes occupy a subordinate place, while quadrupeds, birds, and reptiles are invoked almost constantly. The uktena (a mythic great horned serpent), the rattlesnake, and the terrapin, the various species of hawk, and the rabbit, the squirrel, and the dog are the principal animal gods. The importance of the god bears no relation to the size of the animal, and in fact the larger animals are but seldom invoked. The spider also occupies a prominent place in the love and life-destroying formulas, his duty being to entangle the soul of his victim in the meshes of his web or to pluck it from the body of the doomed man and drag it way to the black coffin in the Darkening Land.

Among what may be classed as elemental gods the principal are fire, water, and the sun, all of which are addressed under figurative names. The sun is called Une"˙lanû'hĭ, "the apportioner," just as our word moon means originally "the measurer." Indians and Aryans alike, having noticed how these great luminaries divide and measure day and night, summer and winter, with never varying regularity, have given to each a name which should indicate these characteristics, thus showing how the human mind constantly moves on along the same channels. Missionaries have naturally, but incorrectly, assumed this apportioner of all things to be the suppositional "Great Spirit" of the Cherokees and hence the word is used in the Bible translation as synonymous with God. In ordinary conversation and in the lesser myths the sun is called Nû'ntâ. The sun is invoked chiefly by the ball-player, while the hunter prays to the fire; but every important ceremony--whether connected with medicine, love, hunting, or the ball play--contains a prayer to the "Long Person," the formulistic name for water, or, more strictly speaking, for the river. The wind, the storm, the cloud, and the frost are also invoked in different formulas.

But few inanimate gods are included in the category, the principal being the Stone, to which the shaman prays while endeavoring to find a lost article by means of a swinging pebble suspended by a string; the Flint, invoked when the shaman is about to scarify the patient with a flint arrow-head before rubbing on the medicine; and the Mountain, which is addressed in one or two of the formulas thus far translated. Plant gods do not appear prominently, the chief one seeming to be the ginseng, addressed in the formulas as the "Great Man" or "Little Man," although its proper Cherokee name signifies the "Mountain Climber."

A number of personal deities are also invoked, the principal being the Red Man. He is one of the greatest of the gods, being repeatedly called upon in formulas of all kinds, and is hardly subordinate to the Fire, the Water, or the Sun. His identity is as yet uncertain, but he seems to be intimately connected with the Thunder family. In a curious marginal note in one of the Gahuni formulas (page 350), it is stated that when the patient is a woman the doctor must pray to the Red Man, but when treating a man he must pray to the Red Woman, so that this personage seems to have dual sex characteristics. Another god invoked in the hunting songs is Tsu'l`kalû', or "Slanting Eyes" (see Cherokee Myths), a giant hunter who lives in one of the great mountains of the Blue Ridge and owns all the game. Others are the Little Men, probably the two Thunder boys; the Little People, the fairies who live in the rock cliffs; and even the De'tsata, a diminutive sprite who holds the place of our Puck. One unwritten formula, which could not be obtained correctly by dictation, was addressed to the "Red-Headed Woman, whose hair hangs down to the ground."

The personage invoked is always selected in accordance with the theory of the formula and the duty to be performed. Thus, when a sickness is caused by a fish, the Fish-hawk, the Heron, or some other fish-eating bird is implored to come and seize the intruder and destroy it, so that the patient may find relief. When the trouble is caused by a worm or an insect, some insectivorous bird is called in for the same purpose. When a flock of redbirds is pecking at the vitals of the sick man the Sparrow-hawk is brought down to scatter them, and when the rabbit, the great mischief-maker, is the evil genius, he is driven out by the Rabbit-hawk. Sometimes after the intruder has been thus expelled "a small portion still remains," in the words of the formula, and accordingly the Whirlwind is called down from the treetops to carry the remnant to the uplands and there scatter it so that it shall never reappear. The hunter prays to the fire, from which he draws his omens; to the reed, from which he makes his arrows; to Tsu'l`kalû, the great lord of the game, and finally addresses in songs the very animals which he intends to kill. The lover prays to the Spider to hold fast the affections of his beloved one in the meshes of his web, or to the Moon, which looks down upon him in the dance. The warrior prays to the Red War-club, and the man about to set out on a dangerous expedition prays to the Cloud to envelop him and conceal him from his enemies."

Similarly, for the Cherokee, the four Winds are spirit beings that function as the Great One's messengers. They are tasked by their creator (the Great One) with managing the four seasons of the year. The Messengers also keep track of the movement of the Sun, Moon, Earth, and Stars, and they mind the winds to ensure that the four winds do not join together at once and destroy all life on the Earth. Posted at the four corners of the Earth, the Messengers are in constant action to seasonal deeds under the direction of the Great One, standing as perpetual guardians and regulators of the yearly cycles.

Cherokee people traditionally honored the Messengers through rituals overseen and conducted by village priests, and a successful hunter brought a portion of the meat he killed to the priest, who would cut it into five pieces. The priest first offered a portion of the meat to the sacred fire burning in his dwelling. A portion of the meat is then offered to each of the four winds by throwing a piece to the North, South, East, and last, the West. The remainder of the meat is then passed through the sacred fire and is then distributed among all the families of the village. Fire is the earthly presence of the Sun, known to the Cherokee as Wiyaha. The Sun is called the

Grandmother of all that lives and possesses omniscience, seeing all events that transpire on the Earth; her counterpart, the Moon, is called the Grandfather of all.

Specific rituals were also performed to appease the different winds at various times of the year. During winter, the North Wind Messenger is given offerings so he will not blow for too long and destroy the Cherokee with cold. The East Wind Messenger must be appeased during the early autumn, when the corn is in tassel and when ears are ready for roasting, so he will not blow too hard and uproot or overturn the corn stalks. Offerings to the South Wind Messenger encourage him to blow sufficiently, for he is the sustaining and nurturing wind that helps all things to grow. Finally, the West Wind Messenger is appeased because he works with the South Wind Messenger to bring rains that water the Cherokee's crops.

Perhaps unsurprisingly, the Cherokee also gave their wind deities personalities. The North Wind Messenger is considered mischievous, and the other three Wind Messengers are always on their guard against his tricks. For instance, the North Wind Messenger will sometimes use his frigid wind to blow between the West and South Wind Messengers to disrupt their life-giving rain, but the West and South join forces to blow the cold back to the North Wind Messenger. During the summer, all three other Wind Messengers work together constantly to ensure that the North Wind Messenger's cold winds do not damage the newly sprouted corn or other young growing things. Sometimes, the North Wind Messenger visits secretly in the night to blow freezing winds at fruit trees, gardens, tender shoots, and water. The Cherokee believed that the Great One would send all four winds at once and destroy crops and punish people who had done wicked things or failed to listen to the counsel of their priests.

The different Wind Messengers also have specific names, colors, symbolism, and countenances associated with them.

The East Wind Messenger is named Kanati, and he is symbolized by the Thunder Bird. The South Wind and West Wind – thunder and lightning – are his children, and he controls time and space. Every morning, the East Winds blows ahead of the sunrise to announce her as she approaches. His countenance is congenial and the East Wind Messenger's color is red.

The South Wind Messenger is named Usawi, meaning "the Light Magician," and his color is yellow. The Great One highly favors the South Wind Messenger, who is always completely beneficial. Together with his twin, the West Wind Messenger, the South Wind Messenger pushes back the North Wind at the end of winter. Thunder is the South Wind Messenger's symbol.

Nuhsawi is the name of the West Wind Messenger, and his pleasant countenance is symbolized by lightning. His name means the Dark Magician. Finally, befitting his often-lethal effects, the North Wind Messenger's color is black, and his name is Yahwigunaheda or "Long Human Being." In addition to controlling the frigid winds of winter, he is the spirit of all the rivers. Because he is a trickster, the other Wind Messengers stay constantly vigilant against his mischief. He has a stern countenance.

In addition to their beliefs regarding the Wind Messengers, the Cherokee maintained a series of seven sacred ceremonies, six of which were performed annually, with the seventh performed only every seven years.

The six annual ceremonies were performed between March and November annually, beginning with the First New Moon of Spring Ceremony and concluding the season's ceremonies with the Great Moon Ceremony–replaced by the Uku Dance Ceremony every seventh year. Of the seven ancient ceremonies, only the Ripe Corn Ceremony survived into the twentieth century. For the Cherokee, the numbers four and seven were considered sacred, both being related to directions. Four represent the cardinal directions, while seven referred to these four directions with the addition of above/up, below/down, and "here in the center." The seventh "direction," "here in the center" was also indicative of the Sacred Fire maintained in the ceremonial hearth. Seven also signified the seven matrilineal clans and the seven ceremonies the Cherokee held sacred.

The First New Moon of Spring Ceremony took place around the first new moon in March, with primary triggers for the ceremony being the first shoots of new grass and the new leaves budding from trees. This seven-day long festival signaled the beginning of the planting season, and the relighting of the Sacred Fire by a designated "Fire Maker." Cherokee people gathered together to dance, and a deer tongue would be burned in the Sacred Fire as a sacrifice. Finally, every home would extinguish the fires in their hearths and re-light them using coals from the Sacred Fire.

Some time around August, when the new corn was sufficiently ripe, the Cherokee performed the Green Corn Ceremony. It was considered taboo to eat the new corn prior to the ceremony's completion. The towns of the nation were notified by messenger when the ceremony was about to start, and as they traveled between the towns, the messengers gathered seven ears of corn, one each from fields belonging to seven clans. Upon the return of the messengers, the chief and seven councilors began a fast that lasted for six days, beginning the ceremony on the seventh day. Again, the Sacred Fire was smothered and re-lit by the Fire Starter, and another deer tongue was sacrificed in the Sacred Fire along with kernels from the seven ears of corn collected by the messengers. After sprinkling tobacco powder over the Sacred Fire, the chief prayed, dedicating the new corn to the Creator (the Great One) and thanking him. At last, all the people were fed dishes prepared from the new corn harvest, but the chief and his council of advisors only ate from the previous year's crop for another seven days.

The lone ceremony that survived to be conducted during the 20th century was the Ripe Corn Ceremony. This ceremony was performed in a square at the town center around a leafy tree that was moved there for the purposes of the ceremony. The festival lasted four days and involved feasting in celebration of the mature corn crop and harvest. The ceremonial aspects of the festival were distinctly and exclusively male oriented. Two key events were a special dance performed by the chief's main lieutenant and a men's dance, both of which were performed while carrying special green boughs. During the dances, women were excluded from the town square.

The Great New Moon Ceremony took place during October and coincided with the appearance of the new moon. This ceremony celebrated the arrival of the New Year, because Cherokee legend held that the world was created during the autumn. Families brought portions of the crops they had grown in their personal field, and activities included dancing and a purification ceremony known as "going to water." In the purification rite, participants were immersed in water seven times, and using a sacred crystal, the priest predicted the participants' health during the coming year.

James Mooney explained the "going to water" ritual, as well as its supposed effects on lovers in the tribe:

"The technical word used in the heading, ä'tawasti'yĭ, signifies plunging or going entirely into a liquid. The expression used for the ordinary "going to water," where the water is simply dipped up with the hand, is ämâ'yĭ dita`ti'yĭ, "taking them to water."

The prayer is addressed to Agë"yaguga, a formulistic name for the moon, which is supposed to exert a great influence in love affairs, because the dances, which give such opportunities for love making, always take place at night. The shamans can not explain the meaning of the term, which plainly contains the word agë"ya, "woman," and may refer to the moon's supposed influence over women. In Cherokee mythology the moon is a man. The ordinary name is nû'ndâ, or more fully, nû'ndâ sûnnâyë'hĭ, "the sun living in the night," while the sun itself is designated as nû'nndâ igë'hĭ, "the sun living in the day."

By the red spittle of Agë"yagu'ga and the red dress with which the lover is clothed are meant the red paint which he puts upon himself. This in former days was procured from a deep red clay known as ela-wâ'tĭ, or "reddish brown clay." The word red as used in the formula is emblematic of success in attaining his object, besides being the actual color of the paint. Red, in connection with dress or ornamentation, has always been a favorite color with Indians throughout America, and there is some evidence that among the Cherokees it was regarded also as having a mysterious protective power. In all these formulas the lover renders the woman blue or disconsolate and uneasy in mind as a preliminary to fixing her thoughts upon himself."

About 10 days after the Great New Moon Ceremony, a reconciliation or "Friends Made" ceremony was held. The primary purpose of this ritual was the restoration of friendships and relationships strained during the previous year, and participants made oaths of eternal friendship toward members of the same or of the opposite gender. These bonds included a pledge to regard the other person as one's self and were designed to reaffirm and reestablish personal bonds within the tribal framework; symbolized mental, spiritual, and physical purification; and unification of the people with the Creator. The Friends Made Ceremony also included the extinguishing and rekindling of the sacred fire, probably as a symbol of the recommitment of faith and friendship. This ceremony was considered among the most profoundly spiritual one in the Cherokee faith.

The Bounding Bush Ceremony is the most mysterious of the seven rites and few details regarding it remain. Although non-religious, the ceremony involved the dancing and feasting common to most Cherokee rituals. Alternating pairs of men and women danced and carried either four-spoke hoops or white pine bough. The dance was led by a pair of men carrying similar hoops with white feathers on each of the spokes. At the center of the circular dance pattern, a man danced and sang within the circle while holding a box. As he passed the dancers each dropped a bit of tobacco into the box. The dance ended at midnight and was repeated for three consecutive nights. On the fourth night, a feast was held before the start of the dancing, which resumed at midnight. This time, the dancers dropped pine needles into the man's box, and as the dancing neared its climax, around dawn, the dancers began individually approaching and receding from the Sacred Fire three times. On the third approach, each dancer tossed pine needles and tobacco into the flames.

The Great New Moon Ceremony of October was replaced every seven years with the Uku Dance, in which the chief (called an Uku) officiated over the nation-wide ceremony of thanksgiving and rejoicing. The culmination of the four-day ceremony was the reestablishment of the chief's, the Uku's, religious and governmental authority bestowed upon him by his main lieutenant. The chief was then ritually bathed by his advisors and carried to a specially prepared circle in the center of the town's square. He was carried to the bath and the circle from a special throne that had been painted white and his feet were not allowed to touch the ground until he was placed in the circle to perform his dance. During the dance, the chief moved slowly around the circle acknowledging each spectator by nodding his head toward him or her; in return, the spectators bowed to their chief.

These seven ceremonies were merely a part of the Cherokee religious system, and numerous other dances and celebrations were performed for specific reasons. But the Cherokee people began converting to Christianity much earlier than many other tribes, and the tribe's priest class was severely weakened by the mid-18th century due to a pair of disastrous smallpox epidemics. Naturally, the Cherokee tried to explain the origins of the diseases that ravaged their population, and interestingly enough they partially blamed themselves. Mooney documented the Cherokee's explanation for disease:

> "In the old days quadrupeds, birds, fishes, and insects could all talk, and they and the human race lived together in peace and friendship. But as time went on the people increased so rapidly that their settlements spread over the whole earth and the poor animals found themselves beginning to be cramped for room. This was bad enough, but

to add to their misfortunes man invented bows, knives, blowguns, spears, and hooks, and began to slaughter the larger animals, birds and fishes for the sake of their flesh or their skins, while the smaller creatures, such as the frogs and worms, were crushed and trodden upon without mercy, out of pure carelessness or contempt. In. this state of affairs the animals resolved to consult upon measures for their common safety.

After each in turn had made complaint against the way in which man killed their friends, devoured their flesh and used their skins for his own adornment, it was unanimously decided to begin war at once against the human race… The assembly then began to devise and name various diseases, one after another, and had not their invention finally failed them not one of the human race would have been able to survive. The Grubworm in his place of honor hailed each new malady with delight, until at last they had reached the end of the list, when some one suggested that it be arranged so that menstruation should sometimes prove fatal to woman.

When the plants, who were friendly to man, heard what had been done by the animals, they determined to defeat their evil designs. Each tree, shrub, and herb, down even to the grasses and mosses, agreed to furnish a remedy for some one of the diseases named, and each said: "I shall appear to help man when he calls upon me in his need." Thus did medicine originate, and the plants, every one of which has its use if we only knew it, furnish the antidote to counteract the evil wrought by the revengeful animals. When the doctor is in doubt what treatment to apply for the relief of a patient, the spirit of the plant suggests to him the proper remedy."

Despite their explanations, the priests' inability to cure the debilitating illness led many Cherokee to lose faith in their powers and convert to Christianity, which also diminished the priests' political authority.

Chapter 6: Cherokee Nation v. Georgia

Despite their determined and legitimate attempts at assimilation, the Cherokee were ultimately forced to surrender their ancestral lands as white settlers pushed west. While President Andrew Jackson framed the removal of Cherokee people from their land as necessary for the advancement of the nation, nothing the Cherokee could do seemed enough to satisfy the United States government. The tribe had done everything asked of it, including changing its lifestyle, appointing a principal chief, and achieving widespread conversion to Christianity, but it would not be enough.

Of all the forced relocations of Native Americans during the 19th century and the various wars fought between the U.S. Army and native tribes, the relocation of the Cherokee remains the best known in American history.

Even before the "Trail of Tears", many Cherokees had moved west and north to places like present-day Arkansas, Missouri and Texas to avoid the hostilities between the Cherokee, British, and other tribes. This was especially the case during the American Revolution, during which Cherokee, Choctaw and Chickasaw all began to voluntarily move west to avoid the conflict. Ironically, by the time the U.S. government signed the Treaty of St. Louis with the Osage in 1825, they claimed the Osage had to "cede and relinquish to the United States, all their right, title, interest, and claim, to lands lying within the State of Missouri and Territory of Arkansas" so the Cherokees and Creeks could reside there.

The Cherokee's troubles began in earnest at the beginning of the 19th century, when the U.S. government settled a territorial dispute between the states of Georgia, Alabama and Mississippi that required not recognizing the Cherokee's possession of lands claimed by Georgia. At first, the government tried to induce the Cherokee to move voluntarily off this land by creating a new reservation in Arkansas during the 1810s. The Cherokees who did head west to that reservation would ultimately become known as "old settlers", indicative of what was going to follow them.

This fracturing of the Cherokee tribe ahead of the Trail of Tears can be attributed to their contact with white settlers, which caused factions to form with the tribe. The differences among the Cherokee were illustrated and defined by the three distinct courses of action each advocated for. One group sought complete assimilation with the United States; a second group sought to adopt some aspects of American culture while remaining a separate and distinct nation; and the third faction advocated for maintaining the tribe as a separate entity and reverting to a traditional way of life. The threat of forced removal caused conflict between the leaders of these factions and disparate responses from the various groups. Most importantly, these differing attitudes towards assimilation with the United States resulted in the Trail of Tears affecting the tribe in several different ways. In addition to those who would die as a direct result of the removal, the Cherokee Nation itself was divided and fractured into bands that settled in several different places. Finally, those Cherokee who completed the journey to "Indian Territory" experienced severe political and cultural conflicts as the tribe settled in this new land and attempted to reestablish its previously well-ordered society.

After gold was discovered in Georgia on Cherokee land in 1828, the state passed a series of laws severely restricting Cherokee rights in Georgia. These laws also authorized the forced removal of Cherokee people from their historic territory. In an attempt to defend their rights to the land, Cherokee representatives cited previous treaties, arguing that the treaties had been negotiated between the Cherokee Nation (a separate and sovereign entity) and the United States. The tribe formed a delegation led by the principal Chief John Ross, and the delegation traveled to Washington D.C. to appeal to President Andrew Jackson and the Congress.

Chief John Ross

When these negotiations failed, the Cherokee sought an injunction to halt the imposition of the repressive Georgia laws. The initial case, *Cherokee Nation v. Georgia* (1831), was heard before the Supreme Court, but though the Court sympathized with the Cherokee's problem, it was dismissed when the Court ruled that it did not have jurisdiction to hear the case. Although the Constitution authorized the Supreme Court to hear cases involving "foreign nations", the Court held that "foreign nations" could not be applied to "Indian nations." In one of the most famous (and shortest) Supreme Court cases in American history, Chief Justice John Marshall wrote:

"MARSHALL, C. J. This bill is brought by the Cherokee nation, praying an injunction to restrain the state of Georgia from the execution of certain laws of that state, which, as is alleged, go directly to annihilate the Cherokee as a political society, and to seize for the use of Georgia, the lands of the nation which have been assured to them by the United States, in solemn treaties repeatedly made and still in force.

If courts were permitted to indulge their sympathies, a case better calculated to excite them can scarcely be imagined. A people, once numerous, powerful, and truly independent, found by our ancestors in the quiet and uncontrolled possession of an ample domain, gradually sinking beneath our superior policy, our arts and our arms, have yielded their lands, by successive treaties, each of which contains a solemn guarantee of the residue, until they retain no more of their formerly extensive territory than is deemed necessary to their comfortable subsistence. To preserve this remnant, the present application is made.

Before we can look into the merits of the case, a preliminary inquiry presents itself. Has this court jurisdiction of the cause? The third article of the constitution describes the extent of the judicial power. The second section closes an enumeration of the cases to which it is extended, with "controversies between a state or citizens thereof, and foreign states, citizens or subjects." A subsequent clause of the same section gives the supreme court original jurisdiction, in all cases in which a state shall be a party. The party defendant may then unquestionably be sued in this court. May the plaintiff sue in it? Is the Cherokee nation a foreign state, in the sense in which that term is used in the constitution? The counsel for the plaintiffs have maintained the affirmative of this proposition with great earnestness and ability. So much of the argument as was intended to prove the character of the Cherokees as a state, as a distinct political society, separated from others, capable of managing its own affairs and governing itself, has in the opinion of a majority of the judges, been completely successful. They have been uniformly treated as a state, from the settlement of our country. The numerous treaties made with them by the United States, recognise them as a people capable of maintaining the relations of peace and war, of being responsible in their political character for any violation of their engagements, or for any aggression committed on the citizens of the United States, by any individual of their community. Laws have been enacted in the spirit of these treaties. The acts of our government plainly recognise the Cherokee nation as a state, and the courts are bound by those acts.

A question of much more difficulty remains. Do the Cherokees constitute a foreign state in the sense of the constitution? The counsel have shown conclusively, that they are not a state of the Union, and have insisted that, individually, they are aliens, not owing allegiance to the United States. An aggregate of aliens composing a state must, they say, be a foreign state; each individual being foreign, the whole must be foreign.

This argument is imposing, but we must examine it more closely, before we yield to it. The condition of the Indians in relation to the United States is, perhaps, unlike that of any other two people in existence. In general, nations not owing a common allegiance, are foreign to each other. The term foreign nation is, with strict propriety, applicable by either to the other. But the relation of the Indians to the United States is marked by peculiar and cardinal distinctions which exist nowhere else. The Indian territory is admitted to compose a part of the United States. In all our maps, geographical treaties, histories and laws, it is so considered. In all our intercourse with foreign nations, in our commercial regulations, in any attempt at intercourse between Indians and foreign nations, they are considered as within the jurisdictional limits of the United States, subject to many of those restraints which are imposed upon our own citizens. They acknowledge themselves, in their treaties, to be under the protection of the United States; they admit, that the United States shall have the sole and exclusive right of regulating the trade with them, and managing all their affairs as they think proper; and the Cherokees in particular were allowed by the treaty of Hopewell, which preceded the constitution, "to send a deputy of their choice, whenever they think fit, to congress." Treaties were made with some tribes, by the state of New York, under a then unsettled construction of the confederation, by which they ceded all their lands to that state, taking back a limited grant to themselves, in which they admit their dependence. Though the Indians are acknowledged to have an unquestionable, and heretofore unquestioned, right to the lands they occupy, until that right shall be extinguished by a voluntary cession to our government; yet it may well be doubted, whether those tribes which reside within the acknowledged boundaries of the United States can, with accuracy, be denominated foreign nations. They may, more correctly, perhaps, be denominated domestic dependent nations. They occupy a territory to which we assert a title independent of their will, which must take effect in point of possession, when their right of possession ceases. Meanwhile, they are in a state of pupilage; their relation to the United States resembles that of a ward to his guardian. They look to our government for protection: rely upon its kindness and its power; appeal to it for relief to their wants; and address the president as their great father. They and their country are considered by foreign nations, as well as by ourselves, as being so completely under the sovereignty and dominion of the United States, that any attempt to acquire their lands, or to form a political connection with them would be considered by all as an invasion of our territory and an act of hostility. These considerations go far to support the opinion, that the framers of our constitution had not the Indian tribes in view, when they opened the courts of the Union to controversies between a state or the citizens thereof and foreign states.

In considering this subject, the habits and usages of the Indians, in their intercourse with their white neighbors, ought not to be entirely disregarded. At the time the constitution was framed, the idea of appealing to an American court of justice for an assertion of right or a redress of wrong, had perhaps never entered the mind of an Indian or of his tribe. Their appeal was to the tomahawk, or to the government. This was well understood by the statesmen who framed the constitution of the United States, and might furnish some reason for omitting to enumerate them among the parties who might sue in the courts of the Union. Be this as it may, the peculiar relations between the United States and the Indians occupying our territory are such, that we should feel much difficulty in considering them as designated by the term foreign state, were there no other part of the constitution which might shed light on the meaning of these words. But we think that in construing them, considerable aid is furnished by that clause in the eighth section of the third article, which empowers congress to "regulate commerce with foreign nations, and among the several states, and with the Indian tribes." In this clause, they are as clearly contradistinguished,m by a name appropriate to themselves, from foreign nations, as from the several states composing the Union. They are designated by a distinct appellation; and as this appellation can be applied to neither of the others, neither can the application distinguishing either of the others be, in fair construction, applied to them. The objects to which the power of regulating commerce might be directed, are divided into three distinct classes-foreign nations, the several states, and Indian tribes. When forming this article, the convention considered them as entirely distinct. We cannot assume that the distinction was lost, in framing a subsequent article, unless there be something in its language to authorize the assumption.

The counsel for the plaintiffs contend, that the words "Indian tribes" were introduced into the article, empowering congress to regulate commerce, for the purpose of removing those doubts in which the management of Indian affairs was involved by the language of the ninth article of the confederation. Intending to give the whole of managing those affairs to the government about to be instituted, the convention conferred it explicitly; and omitted those qualifications which embarrassed the exercise of it, as granted in the confederation. This may be admitted, without weakening the construction which has been intimated. Had the Indian tribes been foreign nations, in the view of the convention, this exclusive power of regulating intercourse with them might have been, and most probably, would have been, specifically given, in language indicating that idea, not in language contradistinguishing them from foreign nations. Congress might have been empowered "to regulate commerce with foreign nations, including the Indian tribes, and among the several states." This language would have suggested itself to statesmen who considered the Indian tribes as foreign nations, and were yet desirous of mentioning them particularly.

It has been also said, that the same words have not necessarily the same meaning attached to them, when found in different parts of the same instrument; their meaning is controlled by the context. This is undoubtedly true. In common language, the same word has various meanings, and the peculiar sense in which it is used in any sentence, is to be determined by the context. This may not be equally true with respect to proper names. "Foreign nations" is a general term, the application of which to Indian tribes, when used in the American constitution, is, at best, extremely questionable. In one article, in which a power is given to be exercised in regard to foreign nations generally, and to the Indian tribes particularly, they are mentioned as separate, in terms clearly contradistinguishing them from each other. We perceive plainly, that the constitution, in this article, does not comprehend Indian tribes in the general term "foreign nations;" not, we presume, because a tribe may not be a nation, but because it is not foreign to the United States. When, afterwards, the term "foreign state" is introduced, we cannot impute to the convention, the intention to desert its former meaning, and to comprehend Indian tribes within it, unless the context force that construction on us. We find nothing in the context, and nothing in the subject of the article, which leads to it.

The court has bestowed its best attention on this question, and, after mature deliberation, the majority is of opinion, that an Indian tribe or nation within the United States is not a foreign state, in the sense of the constitution, and cannot maintain an action in the courts of the United States.

A serious additional objection exists to the jurisdiction of the court. Is the matter of the bill the proper subject for judicial inquiry and decision? It seeks to restrain a state from the forcible exercise of legislative power over a neighboring people, asserting their independence; their right to which the state denies. On several of the matters alleged in the bill, for example, on the laws making it criminal to exercise the usual powers of self-government in their own country, by the Cherokee nation, this court cannot interpose; at least, in the form in which those matters are presented.

That part of the bill which respects the land occupied by the Indians, and prays the aid of the court to protect their possession, may be more doubtful. The mere question of right might, perhaps, be decided by this court, in a proper case, with proper parties. But the court is asked to do more than decide on the title. The bill requires us to control the legislature of Georgia, and to restrain the exertion of its physical force. The propriety of such an interposition by the court may be well questioned; it savors too much of the exercise of political power, to be within the proper province of the judicial department. But the opinion on the point respecting parties makes it unnecessary to decide this question.

If it be true, that the Cherokee nation have rights, this is not the tribunal in which those rights are to be asserted. If it be true, that wrongs have been inflicted, and that still greater are to be apprehended, this is not the tribunal which can redress the past or prevent the future. The motion for an injunction is denied."

However, that wasn't the end of the judicial proceedings. Prior to *Cherokee Nation v. Georgia* being heard by the Supreme Court, the state of Georgia passed a law stating that Georgia residents obtain a license before settling in Cherokee territory (1830). A missionary named Samuel Austin Worcester, who lived among the Cherokee, refused to obtain the required license. State officials understood that the missionaries were sympathetic to the Cherokee resistance to the Georgia government, so Worcester and a fellow missionary were indicted, tried, and convicted by a Georgia court.

The missionaries appealed their case to the Supreme Court, and in 1832, *Worcester v. Georgia* was heard by the Court. Ruling that the Cherokee nation was a separate political entity, the Court overturned the missionaries' convictions and pointed out that only the federal government was authorized to regulate business and treaty-based negotiations conducted within the boundaries of Native American nations. Thus, the Court overturned the Georgia law on the basis of the fact that the states were not authorized to negotiate the terms of use of Native American lands.

Both the state of Georgia and President Andrew Jackson ignored the ruling. One of the quotes Jackson is best known for, "John Marshall has made his decision, now let him enforce it", is an apocryphal reference to this case. While he did not exactly say that, he did comment on the case to a friend, "The decision of the Supreme Court has fell still born, and they find that they cannot coerce Georgia to yield to its mandate." Jackson thus ignored what Marshall had written and moved ahead with the Indian Removal Act, ordering the state of Georgia to forcibly remove the Cherokee. In a stunning and dangerous break with American Constitutional law, Jackson had essentially argued that since the court had no way of enforcing its mandates, the President was free to do as he pleased.

Notable critics in Congress were outraged, including Henry Clay of Kentucky and John Quincy Adams of Massachusetts, who both thought the Act was a stain on American history. They also lambasted Jackson as an ignoramus who had no restraint or respect for the rule of law, in keeping with criticism of Jackson for being a populist. Over the course of his Presidency, critics would come to strongly detest Jackson and derisively label him "King Jackson."

President Jackson

One of the most famous protests came in the form of a letter written in 1836 by Transcendentalist Ralph Waldo Emerson to President Van Buren. Emerson's letter illustrates the degree to which the Cherokees had successfully assimilated into American culture by the time of their removal:

> "Sir, my communication respects the sinister rumors that fill this part of the country concerning the Cherokee people. The interest always felt in the aboriginal population – an interest naturally growing as that decays – has been heightened in regard to this tribe. Even in our distant State some good rumor of their worth and civility has arrived. We have learned with joy their improvement in the social arts. We have read their newspapers. We have seen some of them in our schools and colleges. In common with the great body of the American people, we have witnessed with sympathy the painful labors of these red men to redeem their own race from the doom of eternal inferiority, and to borrow and domesticate in the tribe the arts and customs of the Caucasian race. And notwithstanding the unaccountable apathy with which of late years the Indians have been sometimes abandoned to their enemies, it is not to be doubted that it is the good pleasure and the understanding of all humane persons in the Republic, of the men and the matrons sitting in the thriving independent families all over the land, that they shall be duly cared for; that they shall taste justice and love from all to whom we have delegated the office of dealing with them."

Chapter 7: The Trail of Tears

Jackson's refusal to enforce the will of the Supreme Court was the catalyst that sparked a determined effort to force the Cherokee out of Georgia. On May 23, 1836, the U.S. Senate ratified the Treaty of New Echota by a single vote. This treaty allegedly existed between the Cherokee nation and the U.S. government, but no Cherokee representatives signed it. The New Echota Treaty set a two-year deadline for the voluntary exodus of all Cherokee people from their ancestral homelands; after May 23, 1838, any Cherokee remaining in their historic lands would be removed by military force. Ross reacted as one would expect to the ratification of a treaty that no Cherokees had signed:

> "By the stipulations of this instrument, we are despoiled of our private possessions, the indefeasible property of individuals. We are stripped of every attribute of freedom and eligibility for legal self-defence. Our property may be plundered before our eyes; violence may be committed on our persons; even our lives may be taken away, and there is none to regard our complaints. We are denationalized; we are disfranchised. We are deprived of membership in the human family! We have neither land nor home, nor resting place that can be called our own. And this is effected by the provisions of a compact which assumes the venerated, the sacred appellation of treaty... The instrument in question is not the act of our Nation; we are not parties to its covenants; it has not received the sanction of our people. The makers of it sustain no office nor appointment in our Nation, under the designation of Chiefs, Head men, or any other title, by which they hold, or could acquire, authority to assume the reins of Government, and to make bargain and sale of our rights, our possessions, and our common country. And we are constrained solemnly to declare, that we cannot but contemplate the enforcement of the stipulations of this

instrument on us, against our consent, as an act of injustice and oppression, which, we are well persuaded, can never knowingly be countenanced by the Government and people of the United States; nor can we believe it to be the design of these honorable and highminded individuals, who stand at the head of the Govt., to bind a whole Nation, by the acts of a few unauthorized individuals. And, therefore, we, the parties to be affected by the result, appeal with confidence to the justice, the magnanimity, the compassion, of your honorable bodies, against the enforcement, on us, of the provisions of a compact, in the formation of which we have had no agency."

Nevertheless, the United States Secretary of War, Lewis Cass, explained the treaty to Chief John Ross by simply saying that President Jackson no longer recognized the existence of any governmental organization among the Eastern Cherokee and thus had no obligation to uphold previous treaties. Also, no one would be allowed to challenge the legitimacy of the treaty.

General John Ellis Wool was the commander first assigned the task of disarming and removing those Cherokee unwilling to depart from their ancestral homelands voluntarily. Upon arriving in Cherokee territory, Wool and his command were greeted by a group of Cherokee leaders who presented him with a signed memorial countering the treaty's terms for both removal and disarmament, and in September 1836, Wool attended a council where he learned about the Cherokee opinion toward the Treaty of New Echota. The general would later write that "not one [of the Cherokee]…would receive either rations or clothing from the United States lest they might compromise themselves in regard to the treaty." Convinced that the treaty was neither moral nor legal, Wool asked to be relieved of his command, a practically unheard of act by a commanding officer. He was promptly relieved and replaced by General Winfield Scott.

Wool

Meanwhile, Brigadier General Richard G. Dunlap and his Tennessee troops began building the stockades that would house the Cherokee en route to their new homes in the Oklahoma territory, as well as barracks to house the troops that would guard the Cherokee along the way. By the time authorities were done, over 30 "forts" had been built to house the Cherokee in North Carolina, Georgia, Alabama, and Tennessee before forcing them west. However, in the course of building these structures, Dunlap and his men met and spoke with Cherokee people, and they also became convinced that the sophistication of the Cherokee, many of whom had converted to Christianity and were well educated, did not deserve the treatment they would meet in the crude wooden pens built for their virtual imprisonment. Believing that continuing with his orders would compromise the honor of his men, Dunlap, like General Wool before him, threatened to resign his commission. In response, President Jackson ordered a cessation of all communication with Cherokee leader John Ross.

By August 1837, the state of Georgia had outlawed meetings by the Cherokee Council, so thousands of Cherokee people began to gather at Red Clay, Tennessee, which they adopted as the new seat of Cherokee government. A U.S. government representative sent expressly to convince the Cherokee to comply with the Treaty of New Echota offered only a message indicating that resistance was futile. A British witness to the meetings named George Featherstonhaugh would later reflect upon the accommodation the Cherokee had made toward assimilation and comment:

"a whole Indian nation abandons the pagan practices of their ancestors, adopts the Christian religion, uses books printed in their own language, submits to the government of their elders, builds houses and temples of worship, relies upon agriculture for their support, and produces men of great ability to rule over them…Are not these the great principles of civilization? They were driven from their religious and social state then, not because they cannot be civilized, but because a pseudo set of civilized beings who are too strong for them want their possessions!"

Nevertheless, the Indian Removal Act of 1830 had called for the forced removal of all tribes east of the Mississippi River, and the Trail of Tears began in earnest in May 1838. The removal itself was both physically violent and emotionally devastating. Spouses were often separated from one another, children were torn from their parents, and looters ended up stealing the possessions that the Cherokees could not round up fast enough before their removal.

The Cherokees were forced along three separate trails that utilized both overland and water routes and averaged about 1,200 miles. The forced removal was carried out by some 7,000 federal troops, and those Cherokee people who refused to comply voluntarily with the removal order (about 15% of the estimated 15,000-20,000 Cherokees forced west) were herded at bayonet point into prepared collection points.

As the first three groups left in the summer of 1838 from Chattanooga, they were supposed to be moved by rail, boat, and wagon along what was designated as the "Water Route". However, the river levels were so low that it proved impossible to navigate them, forcing one group to travel by land across Arkansas. Due to illness and a summer drought, that group averaged 3-5 deaths daily.

Meanwhile, 15,000 other Cherokees remained prisoners, and the overcrowding and poor sanitation led to so many illnesses and deaths that the Cherokees still in the east actually requested that they not be forced to move until the fall. Although that request was accepted, the Cherokees were forced to remain in the camps, continuing to suffer the depredations and misery of the natural conditions.

In November, a dozen groups consisting of 1,000 Cherokees each began the trek west, and most of the groups had to endure traveling 800 miles by land. Only one party, which included Principal Chief Ross, traveled by water. This time, too much rain made the roads so muddy that they became impassable, slowing down the forced marches, and the lack of grazing ground did not support the animals that could have been used for food.

As a result, the forced relocation completely bogged down, and about 10,000 of the Cherokees found themselves freezing during the winter months while still east of the Mississippi. One of the survivors would later note, "Long time we travel on way to new land. People feel bad when they leave Old Nation. Womens cry and make sad wails. Children cry and many men cry...but they say nothing and just put heads down and keep on go towards West. Many days pass and people die very much." Another survivor noted that each new day brought the death of a family member, until his parents and five siblings were all gone: "One each day. Then all are gone."

Of course, the Cherokees weren't the only ones forced to endure the weather, since they were being guarded by thousands of soldiers. After Wool had refused the assignment, Winfield Scott assumed command of the Georgia troops charged with moving the Cherokee off of their land. From the beginning, Scott, commonly known as "Old Fuss and Feathers," rightly feared that the Georgia troops would rather kill the Native Americans than see them safely to the "Indian Territory" in present-day Oklahoma.

Sure enough, the Georgia troops treated the Native Americans in a barbaric manner. One Georgia volunteer, who would later become a Confederate Colonel during the Civil War, described the removal of the Cherokee as "the cruelest work I ever knew." This comment came from a man who later saw his own soldiers "shot to pieces" during Civil War battles. One missionary, who had been working among the Cherokee at the time of the removal and chose to travel west with them, said that the removal was conducted without any humane treatment of the Native Americans and that General Scott's orders were largely ignored. In a letter written in January 1839, Lucy Ames Butler, the wife of a missionary among the Cherokees, noted:

"My husband has been engaged in camp, preaching and attending on the sick Cherokees, since they were first taken. He was appointed to serve as Physician in one of the first companies. He also preaches in camp on the Sabbath as they have made arrangements not to travel on that day. We have heard from several companies, and understand they have considerable sickness. Twenty-five in a company of seven hundred had died, when they had proceeded three hundred miles. In another, which numbered about the same, in two hundred miles, eighteen had been laid in their graves. I have not heard particularly from others. When these companies arrive in their new country, the greatest part will be without shelters as they were in this [place], after they were prisoners; and it is to be feared many will be cut down by death, as has been the case with new emigrants in the country. It is estimated about two thousand died while in camp in this country.

Will not the people in whose power it is to redress Indian wrongs awake to their duty? Will they not think of the multitudes among the various tribes that have within a few years been swept into Eternity by the cupidity of the 'white man' who is in the enjoyment of wealth and freedom on the original soil of these oppressed Indians? I know many friends of the Indians have set down in despair, thinking oppression has been carried so far, nothing now can be done. I will mention one person who thinks otherwise; and it may surprise you when I tell it is John Ross, the principal Chief of these oppressed Cherokees. In speaking of the distresses of his people, I have heard him with subdued agitation of feeling, with calmness and confidence say, 'Though for years, the Press has been closed against us, and the few friends we have left, have at times, been ready to think we must sink to ruin unheard; yet I cannot think the United States' Government is so lost to all justice, that our wrongs will not be redressed, if the truth is fairly set before those, who have the power to do it.'

With these feelings, this man has presented himself at our seat of Government year after year; and though false reports, in almost every form, have been circulated against him, and indignities heaped on him and his associates, and withal being told by the highest Authorities of our Government, that he must accept [the] terms already offered, that nothing more favourable would ever be granted, yet the returning Congress has again found him at Washington pleading for his people. It may now be thought as his people have actually been driven from their native country, and one eighth of them already cut off by death, that he will think nothing can be gained by further intercession; but probably, if his life is spared, he will again be seen pleading with Government, for those that remain."

As that letter noted, Chief Ross, who had so fervently opposed the forced removal, had tragically found himself in charge of an event that would result in the deaths of over one-third of his people. In the end, Ross would leave his homeland with the last of 13 groups of Cherokee in

December of 1838, carrying with him the tribe's laws and historical records. Before his arrival in the Oklahoma Territory in late March of 1839, Ross would bury his own wife in a shallow grave along the trail, and she joined an estimated 8,000 other Cherokees in death. Nonetheless, in March 1839, Ross dutifully reported:

> Dear Sir,
>
> We would respectfully inform you that we arrived here on yesterday the 14th Inst & that we are here and do not know what dis-position to make of the public Teams & of the public property in our charge. We have no funds to pay for the Subsistence of the teams & the waggoners & we wish some immediate instructions on the subject. The Agent of the Government will be here today. We will be mustered out of Service and Turned Over to government & we are informed that they have some shelled corn & Some very poor beef for our Subsistence which is unfit for use & from the promises made to us in the Nation East we did not Expect such treatment.
>
> Very Respectfully
>
> Mr John Ross Your Most Obt Sevts
>
> George Hicks &
>
> Collins McDonald

Today the forced removal of the Cherokee is poignantly and somberly remembered as the "Trail of Tears", and in the Cherokee language the event was known as "Nunahi-Duna-Dlo-Hilu-I" ("The Trail Where They Cried"). To a great extent, the incident can be viewed as a predictive event signaling the subsequent course relations between Native Americans and the United States would take. The forced removal is also indicative of the attitudes toward Native Americans held by famed "Indian fighters" like Andrew Jackson and William Henry Harrison. As the President of the United States, Jackson's actions demonstrated his disdain for both the Supreme Court and those who disagreed with his vision for the United States. Also, Jackson's policy toward Native Americans changed the policies of previous presidents, who had encouraged Native Americans to assimilate and thereby become "civilized". Perversely, Jackson's attitudes and actions toward Native American punished those tribes that had achieved the highest levels of assimilation, and although Jackson had left office by the time of the Cherokee removal, his Vice-President and successor, Martin Van Buren, vowed to continue Jackson's policies and appointed all but one of Jackson's cabinet members to serve him as well.

The Cherokee Trail of Tears was not the first incident of forced removal in North America was not the first Native American tribe forced off their land - the British government forced French Acadians living in Nova Scotia to relocate to Louisiana in the 18th century – but their removal had profound effects. Immediately prior to the Cherokee removal, the Choctaw, Chickasaw, and Creek Nations all elected to leave their traditional homelands, though they did so under extreme duress. But with the Cherokee's forced removal, assimilation, which had been the official policy of the U.S. government, was effectively abandoned. Instead, the forced removal of Native Americans from their traditional homelands effectively became U.S. government policy. In the second half of the 19th century, the Navajo people of the American Southwest were forced from their land in an incident they refer to as the Long Walk. Several tribes on the Great Plains, like the Sioux, resisted in a series of wars but ultimately suffered the same fate.

Chapter 8: The Aftermath

The Cherokees tried to rebuild their institutions over the next several decades, but their participation in the Civil War led the U.S. government to again interfere in their dealings. The Curtis Act of 1898 dismantled all tribal governments and institutions ahead of admitting the federal territory where the Cherokees had been relocated into new states, thus eliminating the Cherokee courts and government in the region yet again.

Having already lost their land, the Cherokees were also deprived of their unique identity during the end of the 19th century when the South went about instituting Jim Crow laws. By implementing a segregated society, the Native Americans were naturally categorized as colored, meaning they were treated no better than African Americans. Until the Civil Rights Movement helped secure basic civil rights for minorities, the Cherokees suffered right alongside everyone else.

Today the federal government currently recognizes three distinct bands of Cherokee people. These are the Cherokee Nation of Oklahoma, United Keetoowah Band of Cherokee Indians (Oklahoma), and the Eastern Band of Cherokee Indians (North Carolina). A fourth band, the Echota Cherokee, located in northern Alabama, is recognized only by that state.

Among Native American tribes today, the Cherokee is the second largest in terms of registration of official tribal members and boasts some 300,000 tribal citizens. A 7,000 square mile plot in eastern Oklahoma is home to about 70,000 Cherokee and is not a reservation but rather a federally-recognized sovereign nation. The Cherokee Nation functions with a governmental system similar to that of the United States and includes judicial, executive and legislative branches.

Despite everything they endured, the Cherokee tribe has continued to assimilate to the extent of their abilities. In 1976, the Cherokee Nation drafted and approved a new constitution that allotted executive power to a Principal Chief who is elected to four-year terms by registered tribal voters. The legislative power of the tribe rests with the Tribal Council, presided over by a Deputy Principal Chief who functions in this way much like the Vice President of the United States in his role over the Senate. The Cherokee Nation Appeals Tribunal holds the judicial power within the nation and includes a District Court and the Tribal Appeals Tribunal, which function very much like U.S. District Courts and the Supreme Court respectively. These courts hear cases brought before them based on the Cherokee Nation Judicial Code.

The Cherokee Nation has overcome severe obstacles and setbacks, but the tribe has repeatedly proven that its people are resilient and resourceful. In the modern era, the tribe has overcome discrimination and hardship to establish themselves as not only a successful Native American tribe but as an economically and politically viable entity, fully capable of self-government and self-determination. The tribe has established business ventures and has successfully established a tax system independent of the United States. The Cherokee Nation stands as a model not only for other Native American tribes but for citizens in general, as their resourcefulness and shrewd political acumen has afforded them the chance to thrive in the 21st century.

Eyewitness John Burnett's Account of the Trail of Tears

"Children: This is my birthday, December 11, 1890, I am eighty years old today. I was born at Kings Iron Works in Sulllivan County, Tennessee, December the 11th, 1810. I grew into manhood fishing in Beaver Creek and roaming through the forest hunting the deer and the wild boar and the timber wolf. Often spending weeks at a time in the solitary wilderness with no companions but my rifle, hunting knife, and a small hatchet that I carried in my belt in all of my wilderness wanderings.

On these long hunting trips I met and became acquainted with many of the Cherokee Indians, hunting with them by day and sleeping around their camp fires by night. I learned to speak their language, and they taught me the arts of trailing and building traps and snares. On one of my long hunts in the fall of 1829, I found a young Cherokee who had been shot by a roving band of hunters and who had eluded his pursuers and concealed himself under a shelving rock. Weak from loss of blood, the poor creature was unable to walk and almost famished for water. I carried him to a spring, bathed and bandaged the bullet wound, and built a shelter out of bark peeled from a dead chestnut tree. I nursed and protected him feeding him on chestnuts and toasted deer meat. When he was able to travel I accompanied him to the home of his people and remained so long that I was given up for lost. By this time I had become an expert rifleman and fairly good archer and a good trapper and spent most of my time in the forest in quest of game.

The removal of Cherokee Indians from their lifelong homes in the year of 1838 found me a young man in the prime of life and a Private soldier in the American Army. Being acquainted with many of the Indians and able to fluently speak their language, I was sent as interpreter into the Smoky Mountain Country in May, 1838, and witnessed the execution of the most brutal order in the History of American Warfare. I saw the helpless Cherokees arrested and dragged from their homes, and driven at the bayonet point into the stockades. And in the chill of a drizzling rain on an October morning I saw them loaded like cattle or sheep into six hundred and forty-five wagons and started toward the west.

One can never forget the sadness and solemnity of that morning. Chief John Ross led in prayer and when the bugle sounded and the wagons started rolling many of the children rose to their feet and waved their little hands good-by to their mountain homes, knowing they were leaving them forever. Many of these helpless people did not have blankets and many of them had been driven from home barefooted.

On the morning of November the 17th we encountered a terrific sleet and snow storm with freezing temperatures and from that day until we reached the end of the fateful journey on March the 26th, 1839, the sufferings of the Cherokees were awful. The trail of the exiles was a trail of death. They had to sleep in the wagons and on the ground without fire. And I have known as many as twenty-two of them to die in one night of pneumonia due to ill treatment, cold, and exposure. Among this number was the beautiful Christian wife of Chief John Ross. This noble hearted woman died a martyr to childhood, giving her only blanket for the protection of a sick child. She rode thinly clad through a blinding sleet and snow storm, developed pneumonia and died in the still hours of a bleak winter night, with her head resting on Lieutenant Greggs saddle blanket.

I made the long journey to the west with the Cherokees and did all that a Private soldier could do to alleviate their sufferings. When on guard duty at night I have many times walked my beat in my blouse in order that some sick child might have the warmth of my overcoat. I was on guard duty the night Mrs. Ross died. When relieved at midnight I did not retire, but remained around the wagon out of sympathy for Chief Ross, and at daylight was detailed by Captain McClellan to assist in the burial like the other unfortunates who died on the way. Her unconfined body was buried in a shallow grave by the roadside far from her native home, and the sorrowing Cavalcade moved on.

Being a young man, I mingled freely with the young women and girls. I have spent many pleasant hours with them when I was supposed to be under my blanket, and they have many times sung their mountain songs for me, this being all that they could do to repay my kindness. And with all my association with Indian girls from October 1829 to March 26th 1839, I did not meet one who was a moral prostitute. They are kind and tender hearted and many of them are beautiful.

The only trouble that I had with anybody on the entire journey to the west was a brutal teamster by the name of Ben McDonal, who was using his whip on an old feeble Cherokee to hasten him into the wagon. The sight of that old and nearly blind creature quivering under the lashes of a bull whip was too much for me. I attempted to stop McDonal and it ended in a personal encounter. He lashed me across the face, the wire tip on his whip cutting a bad gash in my cheek. The little hatchet that I had carried in my hunting days was in my belt and McDonal was carried unconscious from the scene.

I was placed under guard but Ensign Henry Bullock and Private Elkanah Millard had both witnessed the encounter. They gave Captain McClellan the facts and I was never brought to trial. Years later I met 2nd Lieutenant Riley and Ensign Bullock at Bristol at John Roberson's show, and Bullock jokingly reminded me that there was a case still pending against me before a court martial and wanted to know how much longer I was going to have the trial put off?

McDonal finally recovered, and in the year 1851, was running a boat out of Memphis, Tennessee.

The long painful journey to the west ended March 26th, 1839, with four-thousand silent graves reaching from the foothills of the Smoky Mountains to what is known as Indian territory in the West. And covetousness on the part of the white race was the cause of all that the Cherokees had to suffer. Ever since Ferdinand DeSoto made his journey through the Indian country in the year 1540, there had been a tradition of a rich gold mine somewhere in the Smoky Mountain Country, and I think the tradition was true. At a festival at Echota on Christmas night 1829, I danced and played with Indian girls who were wearing ornaments around their neck that looked like gold.

In the year 1828, a little Indian boy living on Ward creek had sold a gold nugget to a white trader, and that nugget sealed the doom of the Cherokees. In a short time the country was overrun with armed brigands claiming to be government agents, who paid no attention to the rights of the Indians who were the legal possessors of the country. Crimes were committed that were a disgrace to civilization. Men were shot in cold blood, lands were confiscated. Homes were burned and the inhabitants driven out by the gold-hungry brigands.

Chief Junaluska was personally acquainted with President Andrew Jackson. Junaluska had taken 500 of the flower of his Cherokee scouts and helped Jackson to win the battle of the Horse Shoe, leaving 33 of them dead on the field. And in that battle Junaluska had drove his tomahawk through the skull of a Creek warrior, when the Creek had Jackson at his mercy.

Chief John Ross sent Junaluska as an envoy to plead with President Jackson for protection for his people, but Jackson's manner was cold and indifferent toward the rugged son of the forest who had saved his life. He met Junaluska, heard his plea but curtly said, "Sir, your audience is ended. There is nothing I can do for you." The doom of the Cherokee was sealed. Washington, D.C., had decreed that they must be driven West and their lands given to the white man, and in May 1838, an army of 4000 regulars, and 3000 volunteer soldiers under command of General Winfield Scott, marched into the Indian country and wrote the blackest chapter on the pages of American history.

Men working in the fields were arrested and driven to the stockades. Women were dragged from their homes by soldiers whose language they could not understand. Children were often separated from their parents and driven into the stockades with the sky for a blanket and the earth for a pillow. And often the old and infirm were prodded with bayonets to hasten them to the stockades.

In one home death had come during the night. A little sad-faced child had died and was lying on a bear skin couch and some women were preparing the little body for burial. All were arrested and driven out leaving the child in the cabin. I don't know who buried the body.

In another home was a frail mother, apparently a widow and three small children, one just a baby. When told that she must go, the mother gathered the children at her feet, prayed a humble prayer in her native tongue, patted the old family dog on the head, told the faithful creature good-by, with a baby strapped on her back and leading a child with each hand started on her exile. But the task was too great for that frail mother. A stroke of heart failure relieved her sufferings. She sunk and died with her baby on her back, and her other two children clinging to her hands.

Chief Junaluska who had saved President Jackson's life at the battle of Horse Shoe witnessed this scene, the tears gushing down his cheeks and lifting his cap he turned his face toward the heavens and said, "Oh my God, if I had known at the battle of the Horse Shoe what I know now, American history would have been differently written."

At this time, 1890, we are too near the removal of the Cherokees for our young people to fully understand the enormity of the crime that was committed against a helpless race. Truth is, the facts are being concealed from the young people of today. School children of today do not know that we are living on lands that were taken from a helpless race at the bayonet point to satisfy the white man's greed.

Future generations will read and condemn the act and I do hope posterity will remember that private soldiers like myself, and like the four Cherokees who were forced by General Scott to shoot an Indian Chief and his children, had to execute the orders of our superiors. We had no choice in the matter.

Twenty-five years after the removal it was my privilege to meet a large company of the Cherokees in uniform of the Confederate Army under command of Colonel Thomas. They were encamped at Zollicoffer and I went to see them. Most of them were just boys at the time of the removal but they instantly recognized me as "the soldier that was good to us". Being able to talk to them in their native language I had an enjoyable day with them. From them I learned that Chief John Ross was still ruler in the nation in 1863. And I wonder if he is still living? He was a noble-hearted fellow and suffered a lot for his race.

At one time, he was arrested and thrown into a dirty jail in an effort to break his spirit, but he remained true to his people and led them in prayer when they started on their exile. And his Christian wife sacrificed her life for a little girl who had pneumonia. The Anglo-Saxon race would build a towering monument to perpetuate her noble act in giving her only blanket for comfort of a sick child. Incidentally the child recovered, but Mrs. Ross is sleeping in a unmarked grave far from her native Smoky Mountain home.

When Scott invaded the Indian country some of the Cherokees fled to caves and dens in the mountains and were never captured and they are there today. I have long intended going there and trying to find them but I have put off going from year to year and now I am too feeble to ride that far. The fleeing years have come and gone and old age has overtaken me. I can truthfully say that neither my rifle nor my knife were stained with Cherokee blood.

I can truthfully say that I did my best for them when they certainly did need a friend. Twenty-five years after the removal I still lived in their memory as "the soldier that was good to us".

However, murder is murder whether committed by the villain skulking in the dark or by uniformed men stepping to the strains of martial music.

Murder is murder, and somebody must answer. Somebody must explain the streams of blood that flowed in the Indian country in the summer of 1838. Somebody must explain the 4000 silent graves that mark the trail of the Cherokees to their exile. I wish I could forget it all, but the picture of 645 wagons lumbering over the frozen ground with their cargo of suffering humanity still lingers in my memory.

Let the historian of a future day tell the sad story with its sighs, its tears and dying groans. Let the great Judge of all the earth weigh our actions and reward us according to our work.

Children - Thus ends my promised birthday story. This December the 11th 1890."

The Cherokee Constitution of 1839

The foregoing instrument was read, considered, and approved by us this 23d day of August, 1839. Aaron Price, Major Pullum, Young Elders, Deer Track, Young Puppy, Turtle Fields, July, The Eagle, The Crying Buffalo and a great number of respectable Old Settlers and late Emigrants, too numerous to be copied.

It being determined that a constitution should be made for the inchoate government, men were selected by its sponsors, from those at the Illinois Camp Ground, including as many western Cherokees as could be induced to sign it; their number being less than two dozen out of a total of eight thousand. The constitution as drafted by William Shory Coody, was accepted by the Convention.

CONSTITUTION OF THE CHEROKEE NATION.

The Eastern and Western Cherokees having again re-united, and become one body politic, under the style and title of the Cherokee Nation: Therefore,

We, the people of the Cherokee Nation, in National Convention assembled, in order to establish justice, insure tranquility, promote the common welfare, and secure to ourselves and our posterity the blessings of freedom acknowledging, with humility and gratitude, the goodness of the Sovereign Ruler of the Universe in permitting us so to do, and imploring His aid and guidance in its accomplishment--do ordain and establish this Constitution for the government of the Cherokee Nation.

Article I.

Sec. 1. The boundary of the Cherokee Nation shall be that described in the treaty of 1833 between the United States and Western Cherokees, subject to such extension as may be made in the adjustment of the unfinished business with the United States.

Sec. 2. The lands of the Cherokee Nation shall remain common property; but the improvements made thereon, and in the possession of the citizens respectively who made, or may rightfully be in possession of them: Provided, that the citizens of the Nation possessing exclusive and indefeasible right to their improvements, as expressed in this article, shall possess no right or power to dispose of their improvements, in any manner whatever, to the United States, individual States, or to individual citizens thereof; and that, whenever any citizen shall remove with his effects out of the limits of this Nation, and become a citizen of any other government, all his rights and privileges as a citizen of this Nation shall cease: Provided, nevertheless, That the National Council shall have power to re-admit, by law, to all the rights of citizenship, any such person or persons who may, at any time, desire to return to the Nation, on memorializing the National Council for such readmission.

Article II.

Sec. 1. The power of the Government shall be divided into three distinct departments---the Legislative, the Executive, and the Judicial.

Sec. 2. No person or persons belonging to one of these departments shall exercise any of the powers properly belonging to either of the others, except in the cases hereinafter expressly directed or permitted.

Article III.

Sec. 1. The Legislative power shall be vested in two distinct branches--a National Committee, and Council; and the style of their acts shall be--Be it enacted by the National Council.

Sec. 2. The National Council shall make provisions, by law, for laying off the Cherokee Nation into eight districts; and if subsequently it should be deemed expedient, one or two may be added thereto.

Sec. 3. The National Committee shall consist of two members from each district, and the Council shall consist of three members from each District, to be chosen by the qualified electors in their respective Districts for two years; the elections to be held in the respective Districts every two years, at such times and place as may be directed by law.

The National Council shall, after the present year, be held annually, to be convened on the first Monday in October, at such place as may be designated by the National Council, or , in case of emergency, the Principal Chief.

Sec. 4. Before the Districts shall be laid off, any election which may take place shall be by a general vote of the electors throughout the Nation for all offices to be elected.

The first election for all three officers of the Government--Chiefs, Executive Council, members of the National Council, Judges and Sheriffs--shall be held at Tah-le-quah before the rising of this Convention; and the term of service of all officers elected previous to the first Monday in October 1839, shall be extended to embrace, in addition to the regular constitutional term, the time intervening from their election to the first Monday in October, 1839.

Sec. 5. No person shall be eligible to a seat in the National Council but a free Cherokee Male citizen who shall have attained the age of twenty-five years.

The descendants of Cherokee men by free women except the African race, whose parents may have been living together as man and wife, according to the customs and laws of this Nation, shall be entitled to all the rights and privileges of this Nation, as well as the posterity of Cherokee women by all free men. No person who is negro and mulatto parentage, either by the father or mother's side, shall be eligible to hold any office of profit, honor or trust under this Government.

Sec. 6. The electors and members of the National Council shall in all cases, except those of treason, felony, or breach of the peace, be privileged from arrest during their attendance at elections, and at the National Council, in going to and returning.

Sec. 7. In all elections by the people, the electors shall vote viva voce.

All free males citizens, who shall have attained to the age of eighteen [18] years shall be equally entitled to vote at all public elections.

Sec. 8. Each branch of the National Council, when assembled, shall judge of the qualifications and returns of its own members; and determine the rules of its proceedings; punish a member for disorderly behavior, and with the concurrence of two thirds, expel a member; but not a second time for the same offense.

Sec. 9. Each branch of the National Council, when assembled, shall choose its own officers; a majority of each shall constitute a quorum to do business, but a smaller number may adjourn from day to day and compel the attendance of absent members in such manner and under such penalty as each branch may prescribe.

Sec. 10. The members of the National Council, shall each receive from the public Treasury a compensation for their services which shall be three dollars per day during their attendance at the National Council; and the members of the Council shall each receive three dollars per day for their services during their attendance at the National Council, provided that the same may be increased or diminished by law, but no alteration shall take effect during the period of service of the members of the National Council by whom such alteration may have been made.

Sec. 11. The National Council shall regulate by law by whom and in what manner, writs of elections shall be issued to fill the vacancies which may happen in either branch thereof.

Sec. 12. Each member of the National Council, before he takes his seat, shall take the following oath, or affirmation: I, A.B. do solemnly swear (or affirm, as the case may be,) that I have not obtained my election by bribing, treats, or any undue and unlawful means used by myself or others by my desire or approbation for that purpose; that I consider myself constitutionally qualified as a member of ____, and that on all questions and measures which may come before me I will so give my vote and so conduct myself as in my judgment shall appear most conducive to the interest and prosperity of this Nation, and I will bear true faith and allegiance to the same, and to the utmost of my ability and power observe, conform to, support and defend the Constitution thereof.

Sec. 13. No person who may be convicted of felony shall be eligible to any office or appointment of honor, profit, or trust within this Nation.

Sec. 14. The National Council shall have the power to make laws and regulations which they shall deemed necessary and proper for the good of the Nation, which shall not be contrary to this Constitution.

Sec. 15. It shall be the duty of the National Council to pass laws as may be necessary and proper to decide differences by arbitration, to be appointed by the parties, who may choose that summary mode of adjustment.

Sec. 16. No power of suspending the laws of this Nation shall be exercised, unless by the National Council or its authority.

Sec. 17. No retrospective law, nor any law impairing the obligation of contracts, shall be passed.

Sec. 18. The National Council shall have the power to make laws for laying and collecting taxes, for the purpose of raising a revenue.

Sec. 19. All bills making appropriations shall originate in the National Committee, but the Council may propose amendments or reject the same; all other bills may originate in either branch, subject to the concurrence or rejection of the other.

Sec. 20. All acknowledged treaties shall be the supreme laws of the land, and the National Council shall have the sole power of deciding on the construction of all treaty stipulations.

Sec. 21. The Council shall have the sole power of impeachment. All impeachment's shall be tried by the National Committee. When setting for that purpose the member shall be upon oath or affirmation; and no person shall be convicted without the concurrence of two-thirds of the members present.

Sec. 22. The Principal Chief, assistant Principal Chief, and all civil officers shall be liable to impeachment for misdemeanor in office; but judgment in such cases shall not be extended further than removal from office and disqualification to hold office of honor, trust, or profit under the Government of this Nation.

The party, whether convicted or acquitted, shall nevertheless, be liable to indictment, trial, judgment and punishment according to law.

Article IV

Sec. 1. The Supreme Executive Power of this Nation shall be vested in a Principal Chief, who shall be styled the Principal Chief of the Cherokee Nation.

The Principal Chief shall hold office for the term of four years; and shall be elected by the qualified electors on the same day and at the places where they shall respectively vote for members of the National Council.

The returns of the election for Principal Chief shall be sealed up and directed to the President of the National Committee, who shall open and publish them in the presence of the National Council assembled. The person having the highest number of votes shall be Principal

Chief; but if two or more shall be equal and highest in votes, one of them shall be chosen by joint vote of both branches of the Council. The manner of determining contested elections shall be directed by law.

Sec. 2. No person except a natural born citizen shall be eligible to the office of Principal Chief; neither shall any person be eligible to that office who shall not have attained the age of thirty-five years.

Sec. 3. There shall also be chosen at the same time by the qualified electors in the same manner for four years, an assistant Principal Chief, who shall have attained to the age of thirty-five years.

Sec. 4. In case of the removal of the Principal Chief from office, or of his death or resignation, or inability to discharge the powers and duties of the said office, the same shall devolve on the assistant Principal Chief until the disability be removed or a Principal Chief shall be elected.

Sec. 5. The National Council may by law provide for the case of removal, death, resignation, or disability of both the Principal Chief and assistant Principal Chief, declaring what officer shall then act as Principal Chief until the disability be removed or a Principal Chief shall be elected.

Sec. 6. The Principal Chief and assistant Principal Chief shall, at stated times, receive for their services a compensation which shall neither be increased nor diminished during the period for which they shall have been elected; and they shall not receive within that period any other emolument from the Cherokee Nation or any other Government.

Sec. 7. Before the Principal Chief enters on the execution of his office, he shall take the following oath or affirmation:

"I do solemnly swear, or affirm, that I will faithfully execute the duties of Principal Chief of the Cherokee Nation, and will, to the best of my ability, preserve, protect, and defend the Constitution of the Cherokee Nation."

Sec. 8. He may, on extraordinary occasions, convene the National Council at the seat of government.

Sec. 9. He shall from time to time, give to the National Council information of the state of government, and recommend to their consideration such measures as he may deem expedient.

Sec. 10. He shall take care that the laws be faithfully executed.

Sec. 11. It shall be his duty to visit the different districts at least once in two years, to inform himself of the general condition of the country.

Sec. 12. The assistant Principal Chief shall, by virtue of his office, aid and advise the Principal Chief in the administration of the government at all times during his continuance in office.

Sec. 13. Vacancies that may occur in offices, the appointment of which is vested in the National Council, shall be filled by the Principal Chief during the recess of the National Council by granting commissions which shall expire at the end of the next session thereof.

Sec. 14. Every bill which shall pass both branches of the National Council shall, before it becomes a law, be presented to the Principal Chief; if he approves, he shall sign it; but if not, he shall return it, with his objections to that branch in which it may have originated, who shall enter the objections at large on their journals and proceed to reconsider it; if, after such reconsideration, two-thirds of that branch shall agree to pass the bill, it shall be sent, together with the objections, to the other branch, by which it shall likewise be reconsidered, and, if approved by two-thirds of that branch, it shall become law. If any bill shall not be returned by the Principal Chief within five days (Sundays excepted), after the same has been presented to him, it shall become a law in like manner as if he had signed it, unless the National Council, by their adjournment, prevent its return, in which case it shall be a law, unless sent back within three days after their next meeting.

Sec. 15. Members of the National Council, and all officers, executive and judicial, shall be bound by oath to support the Constitution of this Nation, and to perform the duties of their respective offices with fidelity.

Sec. 16. In case of disagreement between the two branches of the National Council with respect to the time of adjournment, the Principal Chief shall have power to adjourn the same to such time as he may deem proper; provided, it be not a period beyond the next constitutional meeting thereof.

Sec. 17. The Principal Chief shall, during the session of the National Council, attend at the seat of government.

Sec. 18. There shall be a council composed of five persons, to be appointed by the National Council, whom the Principal Chief shall have full power at his descretion to assemble; he, together with the Assistant Principal Chief and the counselors, or a majority of them, may, from time to time, hold and keep a council for ordering and directing the affairs of the Nation according to law; provided, the National Council shall have power to reduce the number, if deemed expedient, after the first term of service, to a number not less than three.

Sec. 19. The members or the executive council shall be chosen for the term of two years.

Sec. 20. The resolutions and advice of the council shall be recorded in a register, and signed by the members agreeing thereto, which may be called for by either branch of the National Council; and any counselor may enter his dissent to the majority.

Sec. 21. The Treasurer shall, before, entering on the duties of his office, give bond to the Nation, with sureties, to the satisfaction of the National Council, for the faithful discharge of his trust.

Sec. 22. The Treasurer shall, before entering on the duties of his office, give bond to the Nation, with sureties, to the satisfaction of the National Council, for the faithful discharge of his trust.

Sec. 23. No money shall be drawn from the Treasury but by warrant from the Principal Chief, and in consequence of appropriations made by law.

Sec. 24. It shall be the duty of the Treasurer to receive all public moneys, and to make a regular statement and account of the receipts and expenditures of all public moneys at the annual session of the National Council.

Article V.

Sec. 1. The Judicial Powers shall be vested in a Supreme Court, and such circuit and inferior courts as the National Council may, from time to time, ordain and establish.

Sec. 2. The judges of the Supreme and Circuit courts shall hold their commissions for the term of four years, but any of them may be removed from office on the address of two-thirds of each branch of the National Council to the Principal Chief for that purpose.

Sec. 3. The Judges of the Supreme and Circuit Courts shall, at stated times, receive a compensation which shall not be diminished during their continuance in office, but they shall receive no fees or perquisites of office, nor hold any other office of profit or trust under the government of this Nation, or any other power.

Sec. 4. No person shall be appointed a judge of any of the courts until he shall have attained the age of thirty years.

Sec. 5. The Judges of the Supreme and Circuit courts shall be as many Justices of the Peace as it may be deemed expedient for the public good, whose powers, duties, and duration in office shall be clearly designated by law.

Sec. 6. The Judges of the Supreme Court and of the Circuit Courts shall have complete criminal jurisdiction in such cases, and in such manner as may be pointed out by law.

Sec. 7. No Judge shall sit on trial of any cause when the parties are connected [with him] by affinity or consanguinity, except by consent of the parties. In case all the Judges of the Supreme Courts shall be interested in the issue of any case, or related to all or either of the parties, the National Council may provide by law for the selection of a suitable number of persons of good character and knowledge, for the determination thereof, and who shall be specially commissioned for the adjudication of such cases by the Principal Chief.

Sec. 8. All writs and other process shall run "In the Name of the Cherokee Nation," and bear test and be signed by the respective clerks.

Sec. 9. Indictments shall conclude---"Against the Peace and Dignity of the Cherokee Nation."

Sec. 10. The Supreme Court shall, after the present year, hold its session annually at the seat of government, to convened on the first Monday of October in each year.

Sec. 11. In all criminal prosecutions the accused shall have the right of being heard; of demanding the nature and cause of the accusation; of meeting the witnesses face to face; of having compulsory process for obtaining witnesses in his or their favor; and in prosecutions by indictment or information, a speedy public trial, by an impartial jury of the vicinage; nor shall the accused be compelled to give evidence against himself.

Sec. 12. The people shall be secure in their persons, houses, papers, and possessions from unreasonable seizures and searches, and no warrant to search any place, or to seize any person or thing, shall issue, without describing them as nearly as may be, nor without good cause, supported by oath or affirmation.

Sec. 13. All persons shall be bilabial by sufficient securities, unless for capital offenses, where the proof is evident or presumption great.

Article VI

Sec. 1. No person who denies the being of a God or future state of reward and punishment, shall hold any office in the civil department in this Nation.

Sec. 2. The free exercise of religious worship, and serving God without distinction, shall forever be enjoyed within the the limits of this Nation; provided, that this liberty of conscience shall not be so construed as to excuse acts of licentiousness, or justify practices inconsistent with the peace or safety of this Nation.

Sec. 3. When the National Council shall determine the expediency of appointing delegates, or other public agents, for the purpose of transacting business with the government of the United States, the Principal Chief shall appoint and commission such delegates or public agents accordingly. On all matters of interest, touching the rights of the citizens of this Nation, which may require the attention of the United States government, the Principal Chief shall keep up a friendly correspondence with that government through the medium of its proper officers.

Sec. 4. All commissions shall be "In the name and by the Authority of the Cherokee Nation," and be sealed with the seal of the Nation, and signed by the Principal Chief. The Principal Chief shall make use of his private seal until a National seal shall be provided.

Sec. 5. A sheriff shall be elected in each district by the qualified electors thereof, who shall hold his office two years, unless sooner removed. Should a vacancy occur subsequent to an election, it shall be filled by the Principal Chief, as in other cases, and the person so appointed shall continue in office until the next regular election.

Sec. 6. No person shall, for the same offense, be twice put in jeopardy of life or limb; nor shall the property of any person be taken and applied to public use without a just and fair compensation; provided, that nothing in this clause shall be construed as to impair the right and power of the National Council to lay and collect taxes.

Sec. 7. The right of trial by jury shall remain inviolate, and every person, for injury sustained in person, property, or reputation, shall have remedy by due process of law.

Sec. 8. The appointment of all officers, not otherwise directed by this Constitution, shall be vested in the National Council.

Sec. 9. Religion, mortality and knowledge being necessary to good government, the preservation of liberty, and the happiness of mankind, schools and the means of education shall forever be encouraged in this Nation.

Sec. 10. The National Council may propose such amendments to this Constitution as two-thirds of each branch may deem expedient, and the Principal Chief shall issue a proclamation, directing all civil officers of the several districts to promulgate the same as extensively as possible within their respective districts at least six months previous to the next general election. And if, at the first session of the National Council, after such general election, two-thirds of each branch shall, by ayes and noes, ratify such proposed amendments, they shall be valid to all intent and purposes, as parts of this Constitution; provided that such proposed amendments shall be read on three several days in each branch, as well when the same are proposed, as when they are ratified.

Done in convention at Tahlequah, Cherokee Nation, this sixth day of September, 1839,

GEORGE LOWREY,

PRESIDENT OF THE NATIONAL CONVENTION

Bibliography

Finger, John R. Cherokee Americans: The Eastern Band of Cherokees in the 20th century. Knoxville: University of Tennessee Press, 1991.

Irwin, L, "Cherokee Healing: Myth, Dreams, and Medicine." American Indian Quarterly. Vol. 16, 2, 1992, p. 237.

McLoughlin, William G. Cherokee Renascence in the New Republic. (Princeton: Princeton University Press, 1992).

Mooney, James. "Myths of the Cherokees." Bureau of American Ethnology, Nineteenth Annual Report, 1900, Part I. pp. 1–576. Washington: Smithsonian Institution.

Perdue, Theda. "Clan and Court: Another Look at the Early Cherokee Republic." American Indian Quarterly. Vol. 24, 4, 2000, p. 562.

Perdue, Theda. Cherokee women: gender and culture change, 1700–1835. Lincoln: University of Nebraska Press, 1999.

Rollings, Willard H. "The Osage: An Ethnohistorical Study of Hegemony on the Prairie-Plains." (University of Missouri Press, 1992)